"Gentle Hands is an excellent addition to the field of massage therapy. It is clinically precise and clear in offering concrete methods of giving a GENTLE HANDS Massage to children. I heartily recommend this book!"

Dr. Brett Smith, Chiropractor

"The earlier you start touching children in healthy ways, the better it is for all of society. GENTLE HANDS Massage shows us how to do it with love and intention in an easy to follow approach."

Linda Henning, Licensed Holistic Health Practitioner

"It's important to touch children from the time they are born, and more importantly, to keep touching them as they grow up. GENTLE HANDS Massage can be adapted for the youngest to the oldest child. Buy a copy NOW and start touching your children again!"

Lorraine Ruskey-DeAndrea, RN

"This book is long overdue! Fortunately, it is coming out at a time when people are more aware of how vital it is to touch, stroke, and connect with our children in healthy, tactile ways. GENTLE HANDS Massage shows you how to so that and enjoy it!"

Carrie Parrish, CPM, MPH

"This is the best book on children's massage I have read! It gives easy-to-follow instructions, has a great reference guide with massage techniques to use for common childhood ailments, and emphasizes the importance of touch."

Wendy Briggs, Director of Dalkeith Day Care Center

"I wish this book had been around when I was having children; however, it has been a treasure to use with my grandchildren."

Carol Wood, Owner of Broadway Kids

This book is dedicated to my husband, Andrew; my children, Angus and Jessica and to all the families and children connecting with each other through touch. Remember, your touch speaks louder than words, so make your hands GENTLE HANDS!

Gentle Hands

A Step-By-Step Guide
To Giving Healthy
Massage to Children

Susan Harley

Published By:
Gentle Hands Book
1151 Evergreen Parkway
Evergreen, CO 80439 USA
Telephone: 303-484-9737
E-mail: info@gentlehandsbook.com
Website: www.gentlehandsbook.com

ISBN: 978-0-615-14584-6

Susan Harley

Gentle Hands

A Step-By-Step Guide
To Giving Healthy
Massage to Children

Susan Harley

v

CONTENTS

Susan Harley

Susan Harley

AN ANGEL TO WATCH OVER YOU

Some people
Come into our lives
And quickly go…
Some people become friends
And stay awhile…
Leaving beautiful
Footprints on our hearts…
And we are
Never quite the same
Because we have
Made a good friend!!
Yesterday is history.
Tomorrow a mystery.
Today is a gift.
That's why it's called the present!
Live and savor every moment…
This is not a dress
Rehearsal!
-Unknown-

Susan Harley

ACKNOWLEDGEMENTS

As I get ready to publish the second edition of Gentle Hands, I am grateful to all of the people who bought all of the first edition books. I am especially grateful to Judith Koch of Institute of Somatic Therapy and the Utah School of Myotherapy who have chosen to use Gentle Hands as the text book for their baby massage classes. It is through the efforts of many that the message and techniques of Gentle Hands Massage will spread.

I would also like to acknowledge my wonderful husband, partner, and friend, Andrew, who believes in me and supports my passion in all its facets and has made it viable for me to write this book. I also want to thank him for the formatting and countless edits he has done for me. To my gorgeous children, Angus and Jessica, who bring me great joy and whose little bodies are the practice ground for many of the GENTLE HANDS Massage techniques.

Susan Harley

To Barry Green for the work he did in order to create the school where I learned the core of my massage education, and for his constant reminder of soft and gentle hands. To Gary De Rodriguez for his study of language and pioneering techniques that have helped me grow and move forward in my life so that I could be here writing this book.

My heartfelt thanks to all of the people, who have contributed their time, help, experiences, and support to this book: Sharon and Michael Hill, Paula Dallywater and Hylton Parker, Carrie Parrish, Anne-Marie Johansen, Janie Saggers, Carol Wood, Linda Graham, Fiona Surtee, and Debbie Paterson.

With deep love and gratitude to my parents who have supported me with great patience, love, and generosity throughout the years, and who have came out of retirement to help me launch this book in the USA. A special thank you to my Mom for all of the nights she rubbed my back for me when I was growing up.

To all of the families who use Gentle Hands Massage—remember, your touch speaks louder than words, so let your hands be Gentle Hands.

Susan Harley

FOREWARD

Touch is universally accepted as a major human need. Why so? Maybe because touch is our primary form of connection. We feel it all around us as we float in the womb waiting to be born. We cry out in anguish as we experience separation trauma at the time of birth.

Since time began, we have tried to stay in touch with our inner being, our inner truth. We have written endless songs and books on the concept of being in touch with ourselves, our heart, and our love. And we have certainly been seekers of someone or something that can truly touch us at the level of our soul.

As philosophical and conceptual as touch can be expressed, the bottom line is that it is still simply the body being physically touched; from the primordial state of an embryo in the womb, to a dying elder being held in embrace of a loved one as they

Susan Harley

pass on from this physical world.

I started my own life as a sickly infant suffering from none other than – asthma. For decades thereafter, I continued to heal wounds, which I discovered were not caused by asthma, but from emotional deprivation from my not feeling connected as an infant. As commonly happens, my own personal healing led me to a career in healing, able to share my experiences and learning with others.

For the last 26 years, I have been teaching others to be alternative health-care practitioners. During these years, I have seen so many grace-filled transformations and healings from the power of touch—touch through massage, touch through words of love and compassion, and touch through like-mindedness.

Sue Harley was one of my outstanding students over the years. In her work, Gentle Hands, she has shared her wisdom and experience for touching your children through massage. She has presented a concise formula and a clear explanation of the non-physical aspects of massage that fill the techniques with the power of human love and compassion.

Remember, as you practice, that it is HOW you do the work that will truly touch your child. WHAT you do is simply the Vehicle to transport and connect your love and nurturing.

In closing, a special thanks to Sue and her staff for this offering, and very sacred and special thanks to all those giving this gift of love to all the new little ones who are coming to take our place in the cycle of life and learning.

With love and respect,

Barry Greene, Ph.D.

Founder and Director

Body Mind College

San Diego, CA. USA

INTRODUCTION

Since I was a teenager, I thought that if I could give a gift to the world, it would be to give every person a massage once a week. Think of the possibilities if we were making decisions about our lives, our families, our work, and our world when we were relaxed, alert and content rather than stressed, exhausted and frustrated. Maybe we would, as a society, be more accepting of people's differences, more willing to respond to situations rather than react; maybe we would be more willing to listen to our children and work with them. I know that in my own life, I have received so much comfort, security, guidance, and clarity through being touched in gentle, loving ways and I desire those benefits for all people. As a teenager, I realized that there was no way I could physically give everyone in the world a massage once in his or her lifetime, much less once a week. Through writing this book, I hope to give guidance, inspiration, and a better understanding of why healthy touch is so important for the growth and development of our children.

Susan Harley

With this book, my objective is to give adults an opportunity to experience both the joy of massaging their children in healthy ways and the deep bond it generates, and an easy to follow, step-by-step guide on how to do it.

Massage is as old as civilization itself. The Greeks, Romans, Africans, Indians, Chinese, and Japanese have developed systems of touch that are continually resurfacing in the field of healing. In the last 25 years, considerable research has been conducted to prove its effectiveness. A large body of work has emanated from the Touch Research Institute (TRI) in Miami, Florida. Massage has been shown to have positive effects on reducing pain, depression, and post- traumatic stress. Work led by Dr. Tiffany Field at TRI has also investigated the impact of massage on children. A study showed that massage therapy stimulated growth in premature babies and as a result, they were discharged from the hospital earlier than usual (Scafidi et al. 1990). Think of the health-care costs we could save by massaging our babies. As more and more research has been done to prove the effectiveness of massaging children, the more acceptable it has become in the mainstream of health care. Many hospitals have programs that teach new mothers how to massage their new babies. I went to an exercise class at the physiotherapy department of the hospital where I gave birth to my children. The babies sat in bean bag chairs and watched their mothers bounce up and down getting get into shape. At the end of the class, we would lay the babies out and give them a massage.

The aim of GENTLE HANDS Massage is to help promote safe massage techniques and create a loving environment where you can bond with your children. With infants, it is a time to uncoil their bodies gently, to smooth out their movements, and to introduce them to the safety and gentleness of touch. When they start crawling and walking, it can be a time of easing the frustration that comes with learning so many new things, establishing a more interactive relationship by making massage a time of games to learn about their body. When they begin going to school, it can be a time to reconnect with them after a day apart, to find out about their friends, teachers,

Susan Harley

homework, and sports. As they get older, it can be a wonderful time to discover what is troubling them, what brings them joy, what they think, what aspirations they hold. If we build that foundation with our children from the time they are little, then they know the feeling of healthy, loving touch and can use that as a guide in their lives. It is my dream to provide families with deep and meaningful connections that last a lifetime. Through teaching people how to touch each other in healthy, loving ways, this dream will become a reality.

DISCLAIMER

Neither the author nor publisher are medical doctors, nor dispense medical information. This book is intended as a reference guide only, not as a medical guide. The information here is designed to help you bond, in a healthy manner, with your children through touch. It is not intended as a substitute for any treatment that may have been prescribed by your doctor. If you suspect that your child has a medical condition, you are urged to seek immediate, competent, medical attention.

Chapter One

THE NEED FOR TOUCH

There is nothing worse than not being able to comfort your child. Trust me, I know. As I write this book, I dash back and forth between the computer, my six-week old daughter, and 18-month old son when they are in need of comfort. My training as a massage therapist has enabled me to research and investigate, through trial and error, different ways of comforting children. For the most part, the techniques contained within this book work are the results of years of research and experience. However, as with the joys of parenting, some things work some of the time, but not all things work all of the time. The key is in applying flexibility and creativity through trying new things when old ways no longer work effectively.

I have traveled, worked, and studied in North America, Africa, Asia, Europe, Australia, New Zealand, Micronesia, and the Philippines. As I studied, learned, and taught, I kept coming

Susan Harley

to the same conclusion; touch is vital to life. It creates the foundation for trust and respect. My travels have emphasized for me that we are born with the instinct and need to be touched. For some of us, that instinct is nurtured and encouraged. For others, it is neglected, discouraged, or abused. Yet, the need remains. Babies who are not touched do not thrive; they become listless and do not develop to their full potential. Adolescents who are not touched act out and look for touch in other ways, many of which are inappropriate. Adults who lack touch in their life also lack vitality, and many times also fill that need inappropriately. Hence, without touch, none of us thrives to our full potential. We arc left with an empty hole that is always trying to be filled. We are social animals that need to connect to other people and touch is a large part of how we connect.

I was saddened to learn how far away we have moved from touch out of fear of law suits and inappropriate behavior, when my daughter came home from her after school program recently, and told me the rule she disliked the most. "The only rule WE HAVE TO FOLLOW is we can't touch, not even our siblings" Meaning, they can't touch their sibling to give them a hug, or in play or in jest or to give a pat on the back and say, 'good job', or 'it'll be ok'. I felt so sad for her, as she is still assimilating our move to the USA from Australia and requires that physical assurance from her brother at times when they are away from home and away from mom and dad.

It is also a direct reflection of how rampant inappropriate touch is spreading as the 'norm' in our world, and therefore, our reaction to it, is to discontinue all touch in order to protect our children. We are paying a great expense for our fear. We are cutting ourselves off from our deepest instincts and desire, our need to connect to one another. We have given our power away to our fears and are quickly losing connections and trust with one another. Please tell me how we can create a healthy, productive society based on that? I strongly believe we must rectify this disconnection in our society in order to move forward with any semblance of healthy relationships between each other. So how do we do that?

It all starts at home. It starts with touching and connecting with our children in healthy ways, so they know what is appropriate and inappropriate as they go out into the world. Knowing and experiencing healthy touch gives them the strength and confidence to stand up for themselves in the event of appropriate touch.

Healthy touch is so important in our world, at all levels of our growth and development, whether we are an infant, toddler, teen, young adult, in middle age or in our twilight years. The power of touch is vital at all stages. A study completed at the Touch Research Institute in Miami, Florida, demonstrated that massage therapy was shown to reduce anxiety and stress hormones in infants. When the therapy was provided by grandparent and parent volunteers, it enhanced the givers' well-being, as well as the children's, while providing a cost-effective treatment (Field, 1995). 1 have found, in my own life, that giving massage is as wonderful as receiving it, as it slows me down, relieves my stress and anxiety, and gives me time to reconnect with myself and others. Being a full time working Mom, it has been a powerful tool for reconnecting with my children at the end of the day.

Furthermore, according to William Sears, MD, pediatrician, national columnist, and best-selling author of, *The Baby Book*, research shows that massage helps babies grow and develop better. Infant massage promotes good self-esteem and brain growth for the child, while also improving digestion and behavior. The interaction also helps parents connect with their babies.

Hopefully, these research results will inspire parents to start massaging their babies and to enjoy the wonderful benefits that come from gentle touch. This book is your guide back to touch, back to connecting; back to the beginning when so many impressions are formed. The techniques described are designed for infants to young children, focusing on touching our babies in healthy, loving ways and on continuing these techniques throughout their lifetime. Massaging your baby will ensure well-being, as well as, giving YOU balance and

Susan Harley

sensitivity and a greater ability to use your hands in a flowing, caring way. The bonding process will begin and allow for a stronger foundation built on trust and respect to develop in the future.

As with all good recipes, these are guidelines to be added to and subtracted from, depending on what you have in the cupboard, your mood, the baby, etc. The same is true for massage recipes. Think of them as guidelines that you add to and subtract from. Sometimes your baby will be more open and receptive to massage than at other times, thus allowing you more time to add different strokes, or to repeat the same one over and over. You also will find that your baby enjoys some strokes more than others, something which is always subject to change. The important outcome is connecting with your child through your touch and thoughts. Let your hands be gentle and soft so they can feel for areas of tension and stress. Watch your baby's face for different responses: enjoyment, pain, or discomfort. Have your intent clear in your mind, i.e. are you trying to relax, stretch out, or calm your baby. Let your focus be on your child and on how you are touching them. If you are uptight or distracted, your baby will respond to those signals. The more you are open to the process of touch and are willing to experiment with it, the greater the possibility for increased connection between you and your child. Let the love you feel for your child come out through your hands, so they feel your love as you touch them in healthy, appropriate ways.

Susan Harley

Chapter Two

LEARNING TO LOVE YOUR CHILDREN

There seems to be an unspoken expectation that you will automatically bond with your children at birth. I saw many friends go through the birth process, only to be devastated because that bond wasn't automatic. One of the most useful pieces of literature I received during my first pregnancy was from the Department of Health in Western Australia, the state where my children were born, in which the following quote was true for me. "It's very important to be close to your baby as soon as possible after birth. Love at first sight won't necessarily follow. It takes time to fall in love. But being close and cuddling gives you and your baby the best chance to get in touch with each other right from the start" (Health Department of Western Australia, 1986).

ANECDOTE

> *When I first saw my baby, all I could think of was how glad I was to be done giving birth. To my shock and amazement, I felt numb when I looked at my baby. There was no feeling when I looked into his eyes. However, as days, weeks and months went by, my heart opened and our relationship with each other developed. Now, I feel a deep love for him.*
>
> *PMS*

LOVE AT FIRST SIGHT?

It takes time to fall in love. We need to create experiences that develop trust. As with any love, we need to cultivate it. Just because we are parents does not mean we are automatically bonded with our children. As with adults, we have to develop that bond with our children and continually nurture our relationships with them. As our children grow and change, so will the techniques we use. Further in this chapter are some techniques to get you started, and over time, to modify.

Here is an extreme example of what happens when we don't touch our children.

ANECDOTE

I had a child come to me who was 2 years old and was still not walking. After assessing the situation, it was very clear that the child had not had any tactile stimulation. So I took a scrub brush out and for the better part of an hour, massaged both his legs vigorously with it. He screamed and yelled, but I persisted. And you know, when I finished, he got up and walked out of that room!

SM

BONDING TECHNIQUES

Bonding with our children at the infant stage is relatively simple and straightforward, yet it can also be a very demanding time. Infants respond to the sound of your voice the best of all, because their eyesight is still developing and they are learning the feel of your touch. So, this is a very important time to TOUCH them. It provides familiarity, safety, and the beginning of your relationship with them. This contact becomes encoded into their body in a non-verbal way, as they have not yet developed language. So much can be said by the way you touch. Soft, gentle, stroking movements enveloped with love and tenderness are the best at this stage. As you uncoil their little bodies, do it slowly and gently, giving the baby your full attention, so they know they are safe in your hands.

Once they start moving into the toddler stage, they experience frustration because they understand so much, yet are still unable to communicate verbally. It is also a time of rapid learning and their patience level can be rather fragile. Often during this stage, massage will be relatively short. However, it is still an important bonding time and can create a safe space for their return. Making massage time into a body parts naming game can hold their attention longer. Ask them where their head is and then give it a massage; ask them where their arms are and give them a massage as you talk to them about what they use their arms for. Use examples of how you saw them using their arms during the day. This dialogue keeps you present with your child, helps them focus on what is happening to their body, and develops a bond in a safe environment. It also gives you a chance to breathe and relax with your child. As you stroke their bodies, reinforce how good the strokes feel, or if you see them cringe, acknowledge that as well. By being in constant touch with your child, you will know your child's body and begin to notice fevers, rashes, discomfort, and other symptoms that may indicate problems or illness, and you will find yourself relaxing as well.

When your child starts going to school, massage can be a wonderful way to reconnect with them at the end of the day. It can be a time to ask them questions about what happened during their day in a relaxed manner, and you can relax with them and listen without other disruptions. Ask them about their teachers, friends, what made them happy or sad during the day; what was their favorite part of the day; how their body feels, if they have any tight spots. Ask them about the tension or pain that they might feel in a certain area; ask them the size of the tension, the shape, color, sound and feel of it. The purpose of all of this is to have a dialogue with your child; to get an idea of how they are experiencing life; to form a bond that comes from being interested in their lives. If you only ask yes and no questions, you find out very little about your child's life. By talking to your child during a massage, it can be less confronting for them to open up, and it can provide a healthy, loving time in which they feel safe to talk. My son is almost 9 years old now. He is at that stage of not wanting me to hold his hand, kiss or hug him in public, yet he still desires it when we are at home. We went through a stage where he didn't want me to cuddle him, especially in our night time ritual of putting him to bed. However, in the last two months, he has started asking for bedtime cuddles again and whenever something is bothering him, he plants his head in my stomach and I rub his back and we slowly move to a chair or couch where I can put him on my lap (he's too big to pick up and carry anymore), cuddle him and continue massaging his back as he gains safety and assurance that he can tell me what is bothering him. It is a lovely stage and what makes it work is my reading his body language that says, "Mom, I need to talk to you and I want to do it in the safety of your arms, as you rub my back." Boys, in particular, find it more challenging to talk about their feelings, so having a safe way for them to open up is vital for their healthy development.

Susan Harley

This bonding technique can be used with your children from the time they can talk, through adolescence, and into adulthood. Your questions may or may not change along the way. **The important part to remember is to be present, to be interested, to breathe and relax; to touch your child in a gentle, loving manner that is respectful to their age and body.**

ANECDOTE

I have three children, 17, 13, and 11. When I had my 17-year-old, I didn't know anything about massage; when my second child came along 4 years later, I was better informed, had read some books on massage, and tried it out. The baby seemed to like it and I found it very calming for both of us. My 13 and 11 year olds received massages from the time they were babies and they still love to receive them. If they are having difficulty getting to sleep, they will call me to come and massage their backs. They are both very tactile children. It's a very interesting contrast to my 17-year old who is very tactile-defensive and uses it as an excuse for everything. He tells people, "Oh, I'm like this because my mom didn't massage me when I was a baby." It's a running joke in our family, and also very true.

DS

Some other simple bonding techniques to use that are touch-oriented include:

- Snuggling in bed;
- Holding hands;
- Hugging;
- Cradling and gazing into each others eyes;
- Smelling;
- Swinging together at the park;
- Rocking in a chair while reading a book;
- Humming a song as you take a walk;
- Chanting with your child in your lap;
- Singing together in the car;
- Gazing into each other's eyes during a still moment;
- Stroking your child's hair as you wait in line;
- Skipping down the sidewalk together hand-in-hand;
- Lightly stroking your child's cheek with your finger.

These are a few suggestions. Let your mind run wild and create your own ways to bond with your children.

ANECDOTE

When my 11-year-old had his braces tightened, it was very painful for him. His jaw ached and he was in a lot of pain and crying. I put him to bed with an ice pack on his jaw and started to rub his feet. He squirmed until I got the pressure right, but once I did, he stopped crying, his breathing calmed down, and he fell asleep. I was amazed at how effective just rubbing his feet was.

DS

Any time you touch your child in a gentle, loving way you are honoring and respecting that child. Children learn how to connect with people from experiences where they feel safe and nurtured. Any way you can convey a nurturing experience with your child will allow continued growth and bonding between you and your child. Have fun and ENJOY being with your creations!

ANECDOTE

I started massaging my babies right after they were born. Now they are 8 and 10 years old and I still do it. They love it and they are also very good at giving massage. So, I receive the benefits twice by being able to relax them and have them relax me. It's GREAT!

JT

Susan Harley

Susan Harley

Chapter Three

FATHERS AND BABIES

When a new baby comes along, especially the first one, men often feel very left out and cast aside, as so much of the newborn's care comes from mom, particularly if she is breast feeding. Plus, before baby came along, it was just the two of you and you had your partner's full attention and now you have to share it with a new baby. This can be a hard time for new fathers. In a sense, they have lost their mate and the baby doesn't need them yet, in the same way it needs the new mother. Many men feel rejected, hurt, angry, left out and lost in this new paradigm of 'family', which can lead to withdrawing, working later than usual, hanging out with the guys or the remote control instead of mom and baby; or it can come out in fits of anger, picking fights, rejecting your relationship with your wife, rejecting the new baby, etc... Does any of this sound familiar?

Susan Harley

Well the good news is, fathers you are needed! The challenge comes in discussing it with your partner. How can you best fill your new role as a father, support your wife and baby, get support and attention for yourself, so that everyone's needs get met? There is no patent answer. It is different for each couple and each couple requires time to sort it out amongst themselves. The key point here is to talk about it with each other and keep talking; keep checking in with each other and trying new things, until you find a way for it to work. Then, just as you are cruising along and getting the hang of it all, feeling included again, baby will go through a growth spurt and the routine will all change, and later down the road perhaps another baby will join the family and the dynamics will change again.

The good news for most fathers is that after the first baby has been born, numbers two, three and all the rest are much easier. While mom is going through the early stages with the new baby, dad is busy with the older children, so the feelings of being left out and rejected don't come into play so much as they once did. Besides, you're usually too busy and tired to notice. However, the fact remains, father's are vital in children's' development. They provide the balance with mom, the yin and yang; the male and female; the loud and soft, the rough and gentle. It is vital that fathers bond with their children at an early age.

There are many ways for new dads to be involved that are very inclusive and supportive and massage is one of the best ways I know and have experienced. Dad can massage both mom and baby. In this way he is connecting to both of them, giving them great support and feeling important in the role as the provider of his family. When I was pregnant, and for several months after I gave birth to both our children, my husband would give me a 20 minute massage every evening. It was the most wonderful gift he could give me and the babies. It gave us a chance to connect at the end of the day, it relaxed us both and it was a powerful way for him to bond with our children. As he took care of me in a way that nurtured and replenished me, I was then able to give back more to him. You don't have

Susan Harley

to be a massage therapist to give a great massage because so much of massage is about your intention, the love you convey through your hands and your willingness to do it.

Now our children give us massages, and we have family massages where the kids and I are all massaging Dad at once. So have faith, fathers; your good intentions and early nurturing do come back to you multiplied.

Rough and tumble, as we call it at our house, is another important way for fathers to interact with their children. When they're babies, it's about getting down on the ground and rolling around with them, bouncing them on your legs and moving their arms and legs so they get a sense of their body and how it works. As they get older, you can start tossing them in the air.

My husband used to hold the kids upside down by their ankles, swing them a few times and then throw them up into the air, flip them and catch them on the way down. The kids laughed with delight and asked for more and more. It was a favorite game until they got too big.

The key for fathers is to play with their kids in ways that engage their bodies, as it develops the child's proprioception, their coordination and helps them to grow into their bodies. It is also a great way to incorporate massage into play. For example, when babies are on their back, you can massage their tummy or legs as you roll them around. When they are on their tummies, you can massage their back, buttocks and legs as you play. Be creative and have fun combining massage into play with your children.

Other ways, beside massage, to include fathers when the new baby arrives are to have dad:

- Bathe the baby;
- Carry the baby in a back pack on outings;
- Take the baby for a walk in a front or back pack;
- Rock the baby;
- Hold the baby and read books together;

Susan Harley

- Hold the baby and watch sports together;

- Put baby in a front pack and wash the car together;

- Get down on the floor and play with the baby;

- Take a nap together;

- Take the baby into work one day and show him/her off to your co-workers;

- Spend time alone with the baby;

- Play 'rough and tumble';

- Hold, cuddle and transmit your love to the baby;

- Give the baby your time and attention.

Above all, give it time; time for everyone to adjust to: having a baby around, being a parent, sharing your partner, creating a family. However, during that 'time', nurture your self, your relationships, and your family and help it grow. As in all aspects of life, families are a dynamic unit. Your role as a father has a huge influence in how your family grows. Be conscious of how you are contributing to your family and what kind of family you are creating. As a man and a father, you are the leader of the family, the guide, the rock of strength and support.

Susan Harley

Respect yourself and your family and participate with your greatness. Help grow and cultivate the future leaders of our world and be proud of your family and what you are contributing to humanity. Above all, cherish your children— you are their keeper for a very short time, so give them your best.

Susan Harley

Susan Harley

Chapter Four

MASSAGE PREPARATION

Before you start to give your massage, there are some things you can do ahead of time that will enable the massage time to flow smoothly and others to keep in mind while you are giving the massage.

- Choose a time when both you and your baby are relaxed, preferably between feedings so the baby is not hungry or full.

- Maintain a warm room temperature as babies lose their body heat faster than adults do and they will relax more easily if they are warm. Have a soft, comfortable space on which to lay your baby. Soft towels or a flannelette sheet works well. With newborn babies, it is best to massage them while holding them in your arms or on your lap as they need extra reassurance, warmth, and closeness.

- Turn the phone off and remove any other distractions.

Susan Harley

🖐 Make sure you are in a comfortable position for giving the massage.

🖐 Have a supply of soft towels within easy reach in case you need them.

🖐 Have your massage oil ready and within easy reach. Pour some oil into a bowl so you can maintain contact with one hand on your baby while dipping the other hand into the oil.

🖐 Keep the back of one hand in contact with the baby and rub the oil between your hands to warm it up before putting it on your baby. This may take a little time to perfect; however, the more you do it, the easier it will become. **Never pour the oil directly onto the baby.**

🖐 Make sure your fingernails are short enough, so as not to hurt or scrape your baby.

🖐 Relax your hands and take a few deep breaths before you begin, and continue throughout the massage.

🖐 Talk or sing to your baby as you give the massage, or have some soft music playing in the background.

🖐 Let your massage strokes progress gradually from a

light to a firm touch and slowly return to a light touch before finishing. Avoid stopping suddenly. Make sure what you do on one side of the body is repeated on the other side, in order to keep balance in the body.

- The quality of your massage will be improved by maintaining your thoughts on your baby and by keeping contact with your baby's body. This might take a little practice as you get used to giving massage. Be patient with yourself. The more you do it, the easier it will become.

- Make all movements connected and flowing. This also requires practice, patience, and flexibility, especially if your baby is moving around during the massage.

- Let the number of times you repeat any movement be determined by your baby's reaction to the stroke; however, try each stoke at least 3 to 5 times before going on to another stroke.

- Encourage your baby to move freely.

- Above all, ENJOY this time with your baby.

Susan Harley

ANECDOTE

When I came home from the hospital with my first child, Madeleine, I was so afraid of her – afraid I would break her; I didn't know how to touch her. She cried all the time and it drove me crazy. I understood then how parents could shake their crying child uncontrollably. One day in particular, Madeleine would not stop crying and I was beside myself, so I called Sue in desperation. She came over and took Madeleine from me. Sue started rubbing her back and talking to her, and in a matter of moments, Madeleine stopped crying and melted into Sue's arms. I was amazing to see the transformation and to realize how my insecurities were causing the upset in Madeleine.

JAM

Chapter Five

THE RECIPE FOR MASSAGING CHILDREN

The joy of this recipe is that it can be done in just 90 seconds or take as long as 30 minutes, depending on the attention span of you and your child. My husband holds the record for massaging our oldest in his restless state - 92 seconds! Play with the recipe, experiment with it, and above all, ENJOY it!

As I mentioned before, following this recipe word for word is not important. What is important is HOW you touch your baby; which requires being flexible, loving, present, and creative. I have split this recipe into the different sections of the body as I found this approach to be more user-friendly with babies and young children. Choose the body part you want to massage, go to that section, and give as many strokes as appropriate for your child. Or, you can follow this recipe from section to section, beginning at their head, and do the strokes in the order they are presented within the section. Add and subtract

Susan Harley

to the massage as your hands and intuition dictate.

HEAD STROKES

Cup your baby's head in your hands. While looking into your baby's eyes, massage the head by moving your fingertips in tiny circles around your baby's scalp.

Use your thumbs and index fingers to stroke the ears, working from the top of the ear down to their earlobe (*Figure 1*).

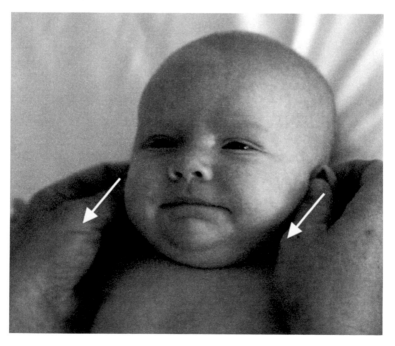

Figure 1

🖐 With your thumbs, start at the centre of the forehead and stroke towards the side of the head (*Figure 2*).

Figure 2

Susan Harley

✋ Gently stroke the sides of your baby's face from the temples down to the jaw (*Figure 3*). Repeat several times.

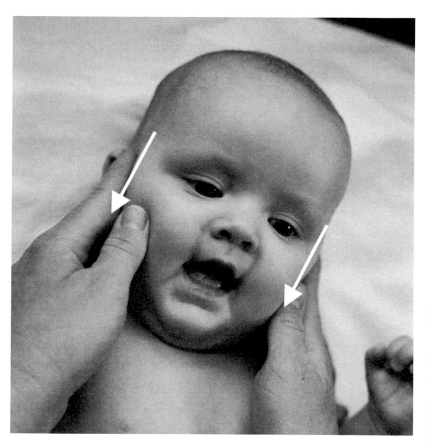

Figure 3

✋ With your fingertips, gently make little, clockwise circles.

NECK STROKES

✋ Use your fingers to stroke from the jaw down the neck and across the shoulders (*Figure 4*).

✋ Using the tips of your fingers, make little clockwise circles on the side of their neck.

Susan Harley

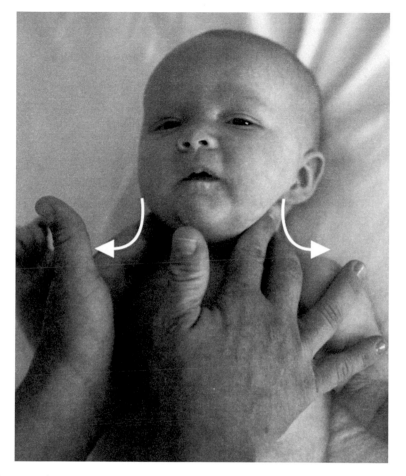

Figure 4

Depending on the size of your child's neck, use 2 to 4 fingers from the back of the neck, sliding forward to the front of the throat (*Figure 5*).   Repeat several times.

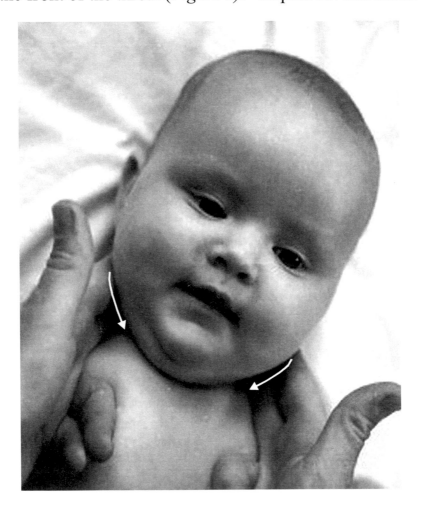

Figure 5

Susan Harley

ARM STROKES

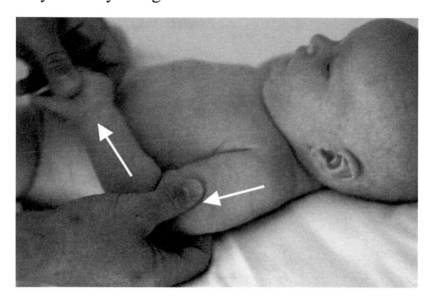 Starting at the shoulder, gently squeeze and release the arm; continue down to their fingers (*Figure 6*). Uncurl your baby's fingers.

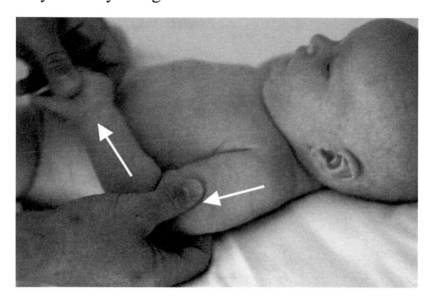

Figure 6

Raise your baby's arm above their head. With the palm of your hand, start at the wrist and make a long stroke down the arm and side of the body to the hip, repeating several times (*Figure 7*).

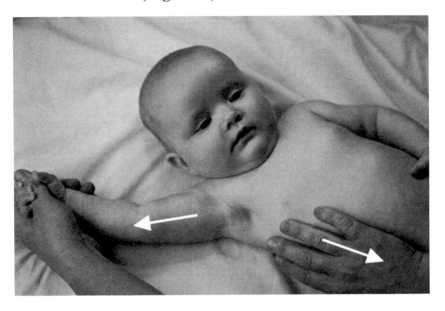

Figure 7

Beginning at the shoulder and moving down towards the wrist, knead the arm by moving your fingertips in tiny, clockwise circles.

Susan Harley

Place your baby's wrist in one of your hands while cupping the arm with your other hand at the top of the shoulder. Slide one hand down your baby's arm and move your other hand to the top of the shoulder (*Figure 8*). Repeat this several times in a gentle rhythm.

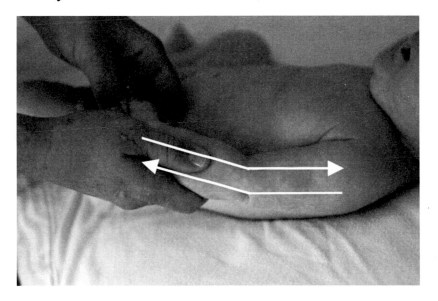

Figure 8

HAND STROKES

 Lightly rest your baby's hand palm down in your hands. Using your thumb and index finger, massage their wrist by making small, circular movements (*Figure 9*).

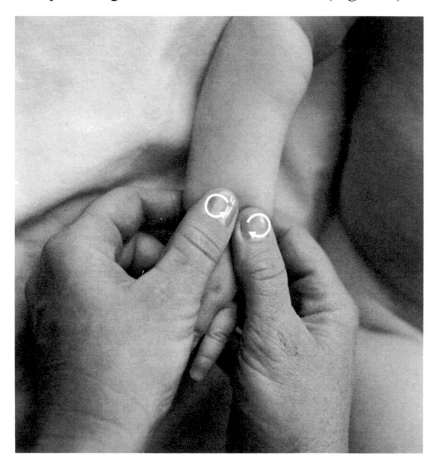

Figure 9

Susan Harley

🖐 With your baby's palm facing up, use your thumbs to uncoil and stroke the palm of their hand, working the entire palm area (*Figure 10*).

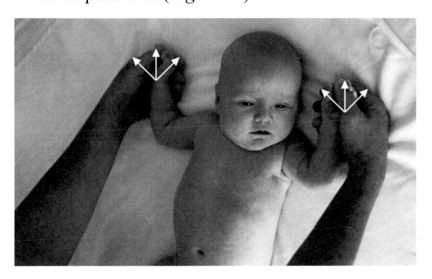

Figure 10

🖐 Hold one of their hands and rotate and stretch each finger, starting with their little finger and working towards their thumb.

Place your thumb sideways in the palm of your baby's hand and close their fingers over your thumb. Use your other four fingers together to stroke the back of their hand (*Figure 11*).

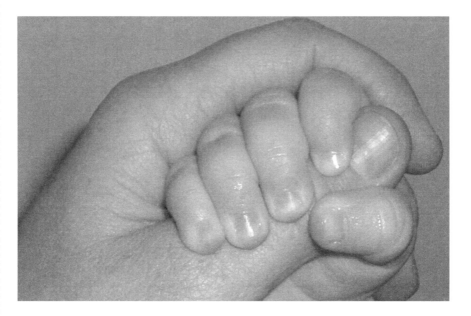

Figure 11

CHEST STROKES

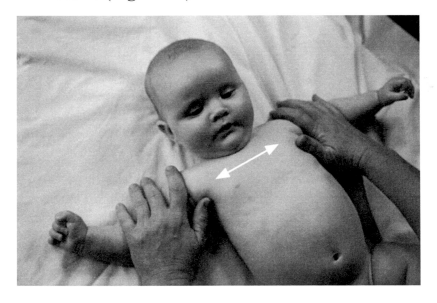 Using your fingertips, massage the chest in clockwise circles.

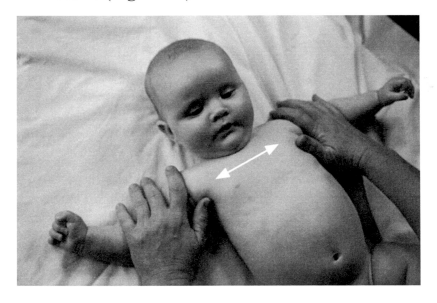 Place the palm of your hands at the centre of the chest and move out towards the sides, extending through the arms to create an opening and stretching of their chest muscles (*Figure 12*).

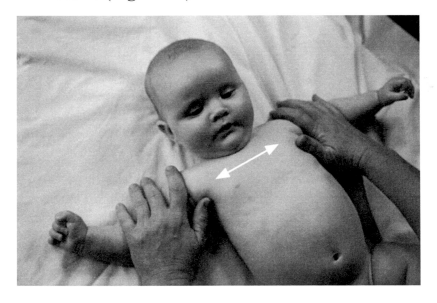

Figure 12

Begin at the side of the hips and using the palm of your hands or fingertips, make alternate strokes close together on the side of the body, working towards the chest (*Figure 13*). Repeat 3 times.

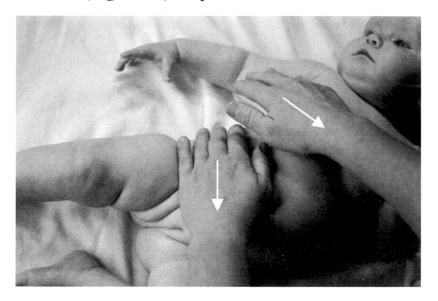

Figure 13

Susan Harley

STOMACH STROKES

✋ Using the pads of your fingertips or the palm of your hand, cross one hand over the other as you make gentle, clockwise circles around the stomach (*Figure 14*).

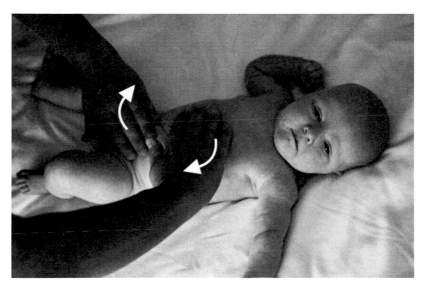

Figure 14

✋ With your fingertips, make tiny, clockwise circles around the stomach area while moving in a large, clockwise circle around the stomach.

✋ Place your palms face down on the centre of the stomach and gently stretch out towards the sides. Then, rotate your hands 90 degrees and stretch the abdominal muscles towards their head and feet.

Susan Harley

Place your hands on either side of their bellybutton with fingertips pointing towards their head. Move your hands out to the sides of the body, around to and down the spine to the hips and back to the front of their body (*Figure 15*).

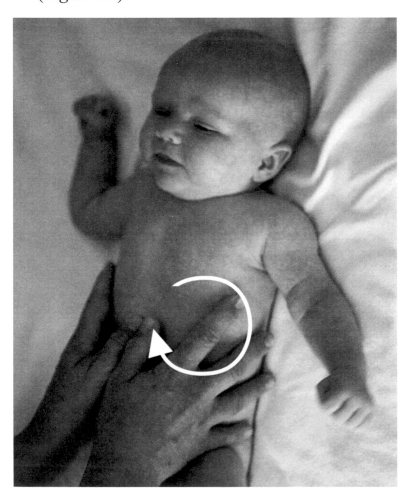

Figure 15

Susan Harley

LEG STROKES

Face Up

🖐 Cup the thigh of one leg in your hand while resting your other hand on the ankle. Stroke down the leg to the foot while moving your bottom hand to the top of the thigh, creating a smooth rhythm between your hands (*Figure 16*).

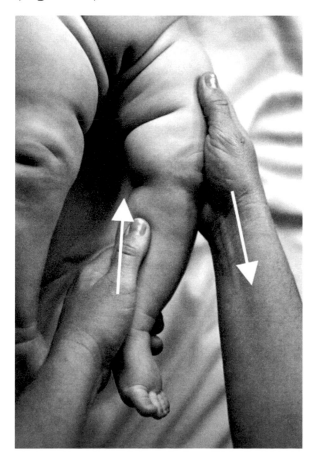

Figure 16

✋ Gently squeeze and release the sides of their leg together from their thigh to their foot. Repeat several times (*Figure 17*).

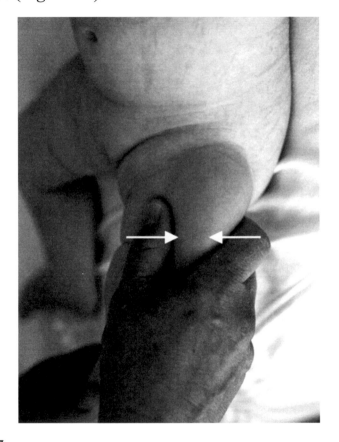

Figure 17

Both Sides

✋ Knead the thigh and calf by using your fingertips and moving in tiny, clockwise circles (*Figure 18*). Work down one side of their leg and then the other.

Susan Harley

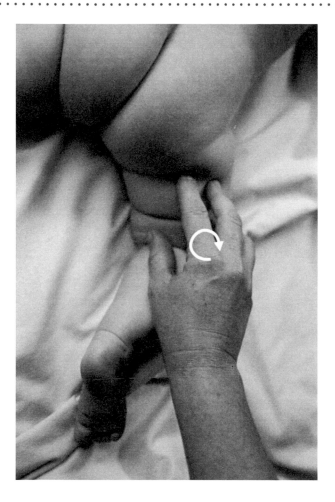

Figure 18

🖐 Hold the ankle in one hand and use the thumb of your other hand to make long strokes from the ankle to the bottom of the knee (*Figure 19*). Begin on the outer side of their leg and work towards the inside edge. Repeat from the top of their knee to the top of their thigh.

✋ Holding the leg at the ankle, use your other hand to make long strokes up and down their leg.

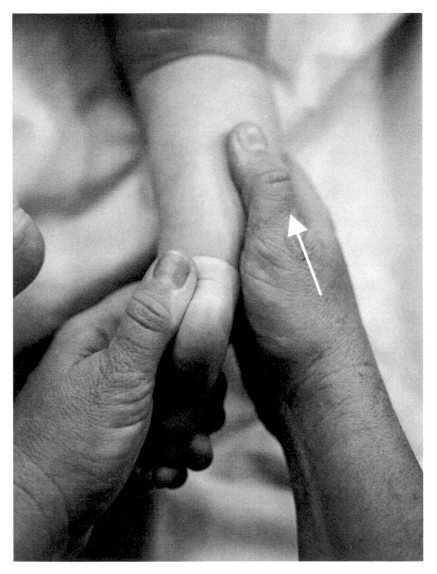

Figure 19

Susan Harley

FEET STROKES

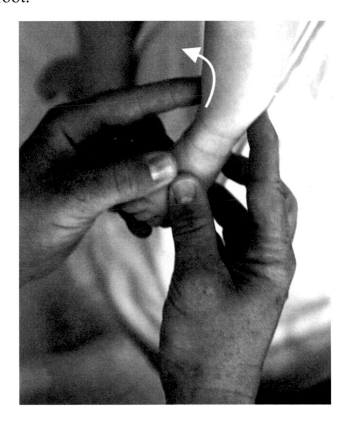 Use your fingertips to massage their foot by making tiny, clockwise circles around their ankles (*Figure 20*).

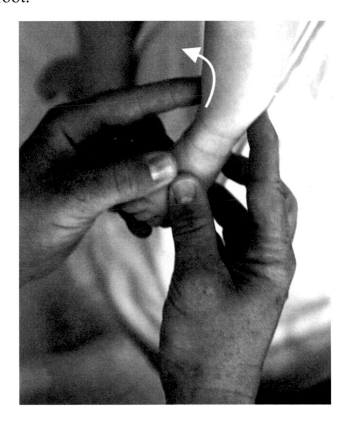 Using your thumbs, make tiny circles on the top of their foot.

Figure 20

With your thumb on the top and your index finger of the foot on the bottom of their foot, make short strokes from the ankle down to the toes, working the entire area (*Figure 21*).

 Rotate and stretch their toes using your thumb and index finger.

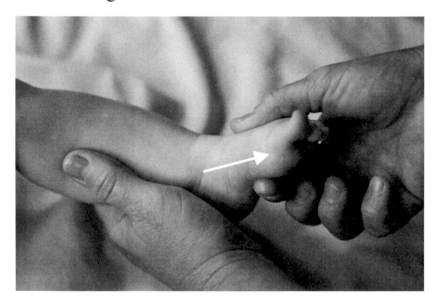

Figure 21

BACK STROKES

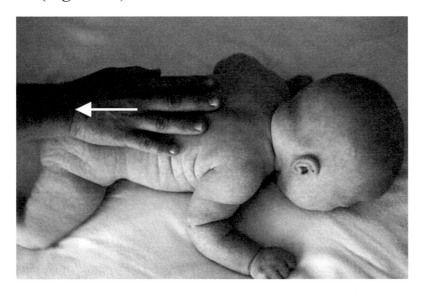 Make long, gentle strokes from the head to the feet (*Figure 22*).

Figure 22

✋ Make a V with your index finger and middle finger.

Run down either side of the spine (*Figure 23*). Repeat

several times alternating your hands.

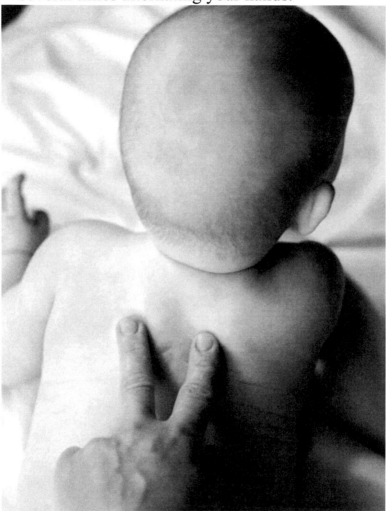

Figure 23

Susan Harley

Keeping your thumbs on either side of the spine, make

tiny, clockwise circles down the spine (*Figure 24*).

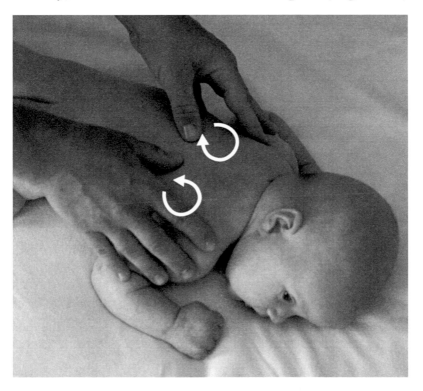

Figure 24

To open and stretch out the child's back, place your palms against their spine and move out towards the sides of the body at the same time. Rotate your hands 90 degrees and simultaneously move one hand toward their neck and the other towards their feet (*Figure 25*)

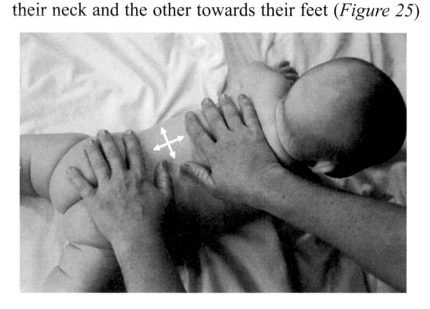

Figure 25

Susan Harley

SHOULDER STROKES

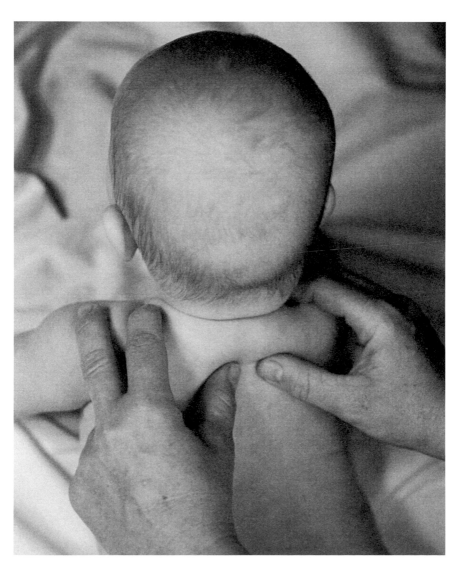

Gently knead the shoulders using your fingertips and thumbs, moving in tiny circles (*Figure 26*).

Figure 26

Smooth out the top of the shoulders using the palm side of your fingertips from the top of the shoulder out towards the arms.

To release tension in the shoulders, use the pad of your index finger and beginning at their neck, press down into the shoulder muscle, hold for a couple of seconds, then release (*Figure 27*). Move a finger-width out towards their arm, press, and release. Continue until you reach their arm.

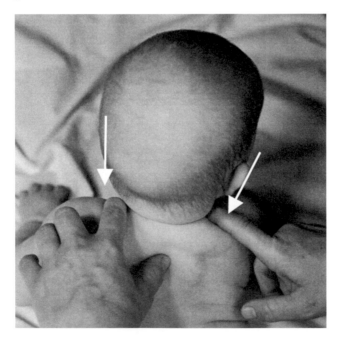

Figure 27

BOTTOM

✋ Knead your baby's bottom by squeezing and moving your fingertips in tiny, clockwise circles around the entire area.

✋ With a thumb on the outside edge of the lower spine, stroke out to the hips, working the entire area (*Figure 28*).

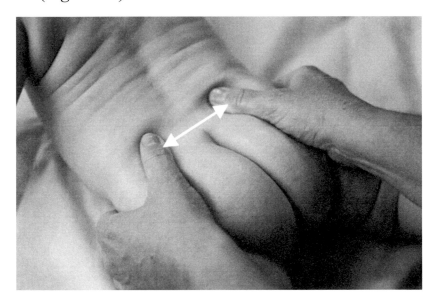

Figure 28

🖐 Place the palm of your hands, fingertips, or thumbs on your baby's bottom and make several, big circles in clockwise and counterclockwise direction (*Figure 29*).

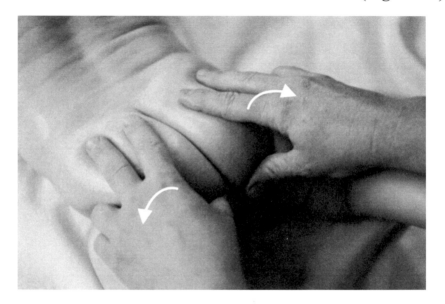

Figure 29

Susan Harley

Chapter Six

OILS FOR MASSAGING CHILDREN

MASSAGING WITH CLOTHES ON

When you massage your children, it can be done with or without their clothes and with or without oil. You may choose to leave your child's clothes on for several reasons:

- the room is too cold;
- they are in a stage in which they do not like to be naked;
- you do not have time; or,
- you might be somewhere where it is not conducive to undress them.

When my daughter was a baby, I massaged her during the day, and I usually massaged her with her clothes on. Yet, my son, as a baby, had his massage after a bath or shower, so I used oil when I massage him. Now that they're both a bit older, they like to mix their own massage oil up for me to use on them. However, if it is late, I just massage them with their pajamas on. The important thing is to connect to them through touch and to be flexible to change as they change, and your circumstances and environment change.

MASSAGING WITHOUT CLOTHES ON

When you massage children without clothes on, there is the potential for a deeper connection, as skin-to-skin contact can transmit more through the nerve endings at the skin's surface. If you choose to massage your child without clothes, oil eliminates the friction of skin rubbing against skin. However, if you use too much oil, the contact will be diminished. A little oil goes a long way. I find it easier to add a little bit at a time until I find the right consistency. If you find you have excess oil, simply use a soft cloth to wipe some of it off. Ideally, leave the oil on your child's skin for 3-4 hours after the massage to give their skin optimal time for absorption; therefore, it is best to massage your child after their bath if that is a quiet, relaxed time for them. My oldest enjoys his massage most after his bath; however, my youngest loves to stay in the bath and gets quite upset when she has to get out, so she enjoys a massage during the day. Remember, each child is different and needs to be respected and treated accordingly. Flexibility is the key!

CARRIER OILS

The best oil to use for children is high quality carrier oil. Carrier oil is a vegetable or nut oil to which you can add essential oils. Carrier oil can be used with or without essential oils added to them, and are very nourishing to the skin. One word of caution, however, stay away from "Baby Oil" as it is mineral oil, which blocks the pores, suffocating the skin. It is tempting to use because it is inexpensive and smells good; however, it is not nourishing to the skin.

There are several carrier oils from which to choose:

- *Sweet Almond Oil*: This is an emollient and will nourish, rejuvenate, and soften the skin; it is light and easily absorbed.

🖐 *Jojoba Oil*: This liquid wax contains nutrients which feed the skin. Although easily absorbed, it is rather expensive.

🖐 *Grape Seed Oil*: A great carrier oil, as it is light. It penetrates the skin quickly and doesn't smell; however, it can stain clothes, towels, sheets, etc.

🖐 *Olive Oil*: This heavier oil is good for the skin; however, it does smell.

🖐 *Canola Oil*: This oil is light-weight, readily absorbed by the skin, and stores well.

🖐 *Calendula Infused Oil*: Calendula flowers are soaked in almond or safflower oil, and then strained. It is especially good for nappy rash or skin lesions.

🖐 *Peach Kernel Oil*: Light oil, easily absorbed by the skin, it is commonly used as a facial massage oil. A little bit goes a long way.

🖐 *Apricot Kernel Oil*: This is fine oil, with a nice texture and is excellent in skin care as it is high in vitamin A.

Beware of cheap prices, as this can signal that many oils have been pressed together. **Some people have allergic reactions to certain oils; therefore, try a tiny amount first on a patch of skin and wait 30 minutes to see if there is a reaction, such as a rash, inflammation, or other irritations. If a reaction occurs, do not use that oil, try another one.**

Carrier oils may be blended together for two reasons. Firstly, blends allow different qualities from oils to come together to enrich the skin. Secondly, blends can be created to nurture different types of skin.

Here are some samples of different blends to use for massage.

Standard blend (100 ml example)

Almond Oil:	45 ml
Peach Kernel Oil:	50 ml
Jojoba Oil:	5 ml

Light blend (100 ml example)

| Almond Oil: | 50 ml |
| Peach Kernel Oil: | 50 ml |

Rich blend for drier skins or chaffing: (150 ml example)

Almond Oil: 70 ml

Jojoba Oil: 30 ml

Calendula Infused Oil: 50 ml

ESSENTIAL OILS

Essential oils are derived from plants in high concentrations and need to be diluted with carrier oils in order to use them on the skin. The scent of the oils and penetration through the skin, via massage and baths, can actually alter moods and provide therapeutic, medicinal effects. There are several schools of thought on how much essential oil to use in carrier oils for children under 4 years of age. On the low end, it is recommended to use 2-5 drops of essential oil/100ml.

On the high end, and commonly practiced, it is recommended to use 25 drops of essential oil/100ml. I use the middle range of 6-8 drops for babies 0-5 months old, 12-15 drops of essential oil/100ml for children 6 months to 4 years of age, and increase

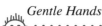

to 25 drops of essential oil/100ml when children are 4 years of age and older. Mild essential oils are best for children.

Good essential oils to use with children include:

- *Chamomile*: An excellent calming and soothing oil.

- *Lavender*: A very important and versatile essential oil; excellent in massage oils as it heals and moisturizes the skin, and calms and soothes the mind.

- *Tangerine*: Used to soothe, calm, sedate, and ease nervous tension, upset stomachs, and colic.

- *Neroli*: Derived from the sweet-scented flowers of citrus, it is quietly soothing, calming, and sedating.

- *Mandarin*: Expressed from the peel of mandarins, it is good for stomach upsets or colic and has a calming and soothing effect as well.

The following dilution of essential oils into carrier oils is recommended:

Dilution for a Baby

	Carrier Oil	Essential Oil
Birth to 5 months	100 ml	6-8 drops

Dilution for Children

	Carrier Oil	Essential Oil
6 months to 4 years	100 ml	12-15 drops
4 years and older	100 ml	25 drops

Chapter Seven

STRETCHES AND MOVEMENTS FOR BABIES

After being curled up in the womb for nine months, babies like to be wrapped and held close for the first few months after birth, as they adjust to the physical world. There are some simple stretches you can do with them to introduce and encourage them to uncoil. I find doing them during a diaper/nappy change is a good time, or when you're playing with them on the bed or floor. Whenever you do it, make sure your baby is relaxed. It makes it more fun for both of you to sing a song or to make it a game by counting in rhyme.

ANECTODE

In my gymbaroo class, I had a mom with a baby with poor muscle tone, delayed movement, and who was slow getting mobile. I suggested to her that she massage the baby each day, working firmly and stretching the limbs. Each week there was marked improvement and the baby is now crawling without difficulty.

DP

Susan Harley

Hold the wrists and cross them over the chest (*Figure 30)*, then straighten them out to their sides, alternating which arm is on top (*Figure 31*). Repeat 5-10 times.

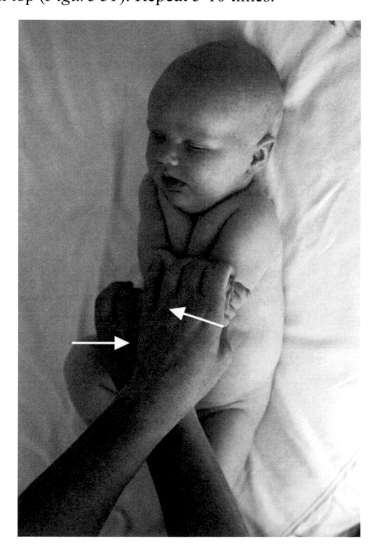

Figure 30

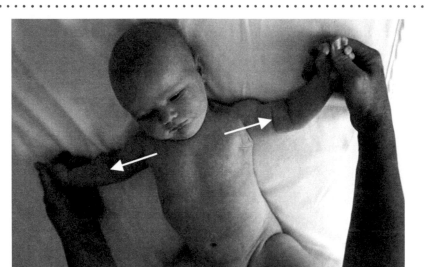

Figure 31

While still holding onto their wrists, lift their arms up above their shoulders and back down to their sides (*Figure 32*). Repeat 5-10 times.

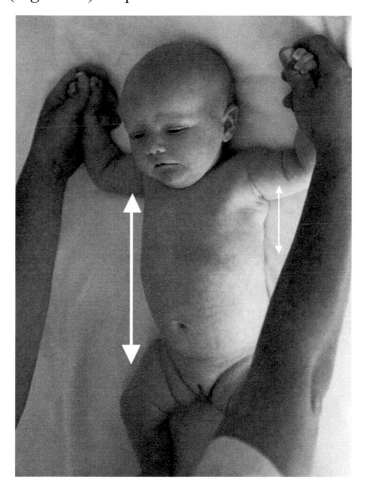

Figure 32

With one hand holding one wrist and the other hand holding the opposite ankle, bring the hand and foot together to the centre of the baby's body (*Figure 33*). Repeat 5-10 times, and then repeat for the opposite diagonal.

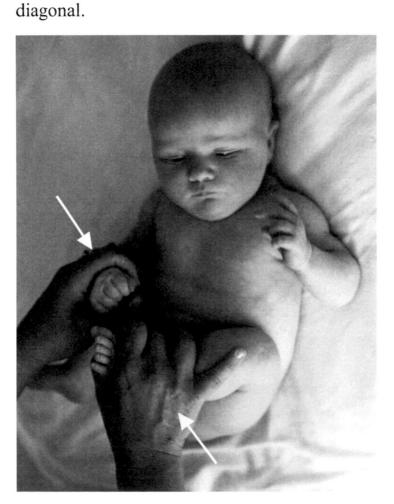

Figure 33

Susan Harley

✋ Hold both feet by the ankles and cross the feet back and forth over each other, alternating which leg is on top (*Figure 34*). Repeat 5-10 times.

Figure 34

While still holding your thumb on the bottom of each foot, push their knees gently up towards their stomach. Repeat 5-10 times. On the last push, rest their knees on their stomach and gently rock their hips from side to side several times (*Figure 35*).

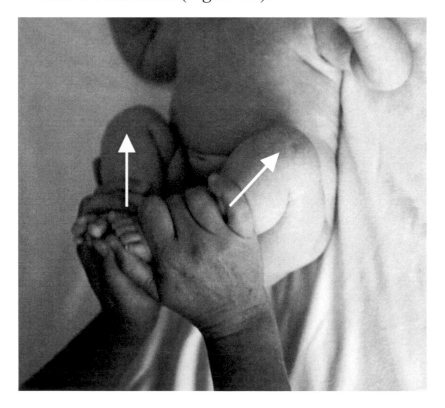

Figure 35

Susan Harley

Chapter Eight

TOUCH TIPS

"As part of the alternative medicine movement, massage therapy has recently received empirical support for facilitating growth, reducing pain, increasing alertness, diminishing depression, and enhancing immune function in infants" as described in a study by Dr. Tiffany Field (Field, 1998).

There are several simple massage techniques that can be of great help for calming and relaxing an upset and unhappy baby. Their upset and discomfort may be caused by a number of conditions. Here are some common conditions massage can help alleviate.

COLIC

Colic is caused by spasms in the intestines and can be quite painful for babies. It often requires trial and error to identify which position will work best, and that can change each time your baby has a bout of colic.

Susan Harley

Try the following positions and techniques:

- ✋ Lay your baby on their back; rub their abdomen in clockwise, circular motions.

- ✋ Lay your baby face down on your forearm with their head cradled in your elbow. Gently rock your baby in your arms while patting and making clockwise circles with your hand on your baby's tummy (*Figure 36*).

Figure 36

Susan Harley

COMMON COLD

Tapotement is light tapping performed with various parts of the hand. For babies and children, try using the pads of your fingertips or palms of your hands and tap lightly, in a rapid rhythm, like you would play a drum (*Figure 37*). This can be done on their chest and back to help break up mucus and congestion.

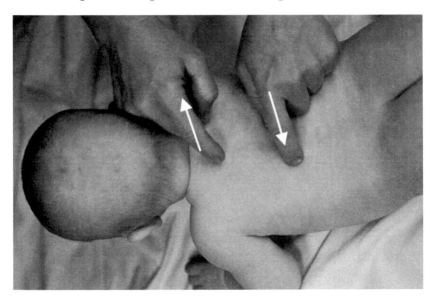

Figure 37

For sinus relief, use your thumb or index finger and stroke from the bottom of child's eyes down to the bottom of their nose and stroke from the bottom of the nose out to their jaw (*Figure 38*).

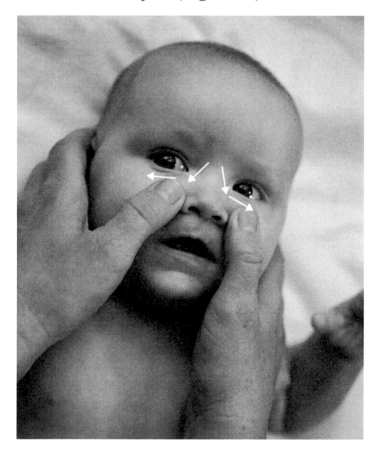

Figure 38

Susan Harley

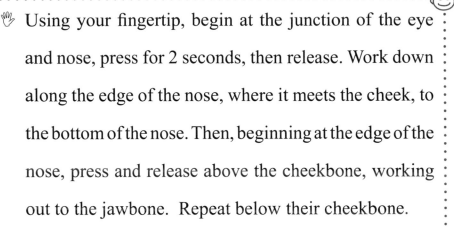

Using your fingertip, begin at the junction of the eye and nose, press for 2 seconds, then release. Work down along the edge of the nose, where it meets the cheek, to the bottom of the nose. Then, beginning at the edge of the nose, press and release above the cheekbone, working out to the jawbone. Repeat below their cheekbone.

CONSTIPATION

Constipation is the infrequent or difficult movement of the bowels. Bottle-fed babies tend to experience this more than breast-fed babies. The feces moves out of their intestine from right to left, so by massaging the abdomen in a clockwise direction (right to left), the intestinal action is aided in doing its job and relief is brought to your baby. This circular motion is most effective when continued for 10 minutes or more.

CRADLE CAP

Cradle Cap is the build-up of whitish to yellowish scales on your baby's scalp, eyebrows, and skin folds of their ears. It can be caused by the lack of stimulation to their scalp, or by soap and shampoo not getting thoroughly rinsed out of your baby's hair. To treat cradle cap, gently massage oil into your baby's scalp and leave on overnight. This will loosen the scales which can then be removed using a fine-tooth comb through their hair; or gently massage their scalp with your fingertips and lightly pick or rub off the scales. Be careful not to pick at areas that haven't loosened up as this can cause bleeding and infection.

When you next wash your baby's hair, be sure to rinse it thoroughly. After your baby's hair is dry, use a soft brush to brush their hair and to stimulate their scalp.

CRYING

Crying is often caused by:

- Dirty nappies/diapers
- Hunger
- Tiredness
- Illness
- Need for attention
- Frustration

Susan Harley

As you learn what your baby's cries mean, it will be easier to establish what you need to do. After you have checked the above conditions in your baby, they may still be crying and need to be soothed. Try the following:

- Hold your baby against your chest and stroke their back in clockwise circles, alternating with long strokes from head to bottom while gently rocking or walking.

- While walking, place your baby's tummy on your shoulder and gently pat their back.

- Lie your baby face down on your forearm with their head cradled in your elbow. Gently rock your baby in your arms (*Figure 39*).

- Hold your baby against your chest and stroke their back in clockwise circles, alternating with long strokes from head to bottom while gently rocking or walking.

- Lie down on the bed and place your baby face down so their tummy is resting on your tummy. Take nice, deep breaths; relax, and massage your baby's back in clockwise circles.

- Gently stroke the sides of your baby's face and say their

name over and over, make eye contact, and reassure your baby during this time.

While holding your baby close, connect with their breathing, and as you do so, melt your bodies together so your baby feels the safety and comfort of your arms.

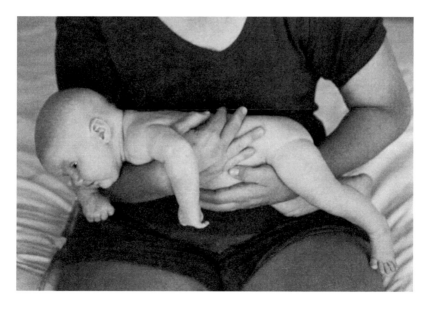

Figure 39

Susan Harley

DIAPER/NAPPY CHANGES

After living in the safe confines of the womb, the outside world can come as a rude shock to newborn babies. This can happen even more so when their body is uncoiled and exposed for a diaper change. To alleviate the trauma, and to comfort your baby, simply gather their hands in your hand and place them on their tummy. Hold them there and talk to your baby so they know you are still there. This way, they feel protected as you change them. As they get more comfortable with being in the physical world, they will lose the need to be coiled up and will lie on their back and kick happily while you change them.

DIARRHOEA

Diarrhea is the frequent elimination of the feces. Babies often experience this condition during teething. To slow down the elimination, massage the abdomen in a counter-clockwise motion (*Figure 40*). For effective results, this massage should be continued for a minimum of 10 minutes.

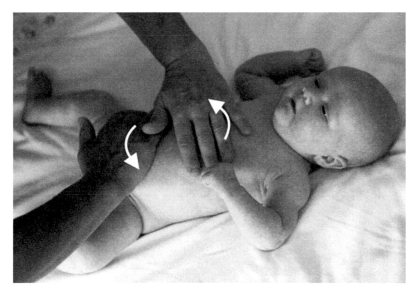

Figure 40

FLATULENCE/GAS

Flatulence is an excessive amount of gas in the alimentary canal, causing uncomfortable distension. The aim is to help the gas out, as it is very uncomfortable for babies, and the process of eliminating this gas is a new and uncomfortable experience as well. Try the following techniques to help eliminate gas.

 Susan Harley

- Place your baby's tummy over your shoulder and gently pat their back in an upward motion.

- Hold your baby's feet and gently push their legs up towards their tummy, as their knees bend. Slowly straighten them out (*Figure 41*). Repeat several times.

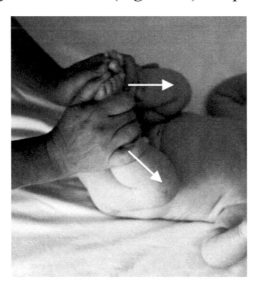

Figure 41

- To help move gas out of baby's tummy, massage baby's tummy in clockwise circles for 5-10 minutes.

- Firmly massage your baby's lower back on the spin area in a clockwise motion.

- Sit down, place your baby face down across your legs, and pat their back.

🖐 Either sitting or standing, hold your baby against your chest and gently bounce back and forth while patting their back in an upward motion.

🖐 Lay your baby face down on your forearm with their head cradled in your elbow. Gently rock your baby in your arms while patting and making clockwise circles with your left hand on your baby's tummy (*Figure 42*).

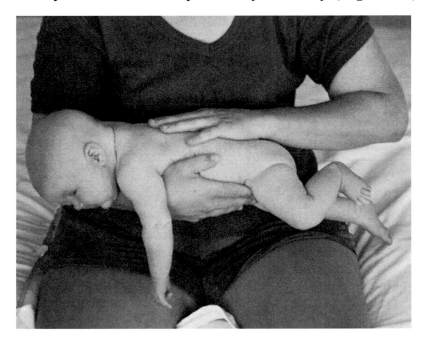

Figure 42

Susan Harley

TEETHING

During teething, the gums become swollen and tender as the new teeth move up and down inside their gum, drilling their way through. It can be a very painful time for many babies. Rashes often develop on their cheeks and chin. Rashes can also increase on their bottoms as much of their fluid is drooling out of their mouth; as a result, their urine is more concentrated. Before your baby has many teeth, you can put your clean finger in their mouth and rub their upper and lower jaw. You may find the baby starts gnawing on your finger, as the rubbing is feeling good and relieving the pressure. As they get more and more teeth, this can be a riskier proposition. Giving your baby rusks or cold teething rings can help, as can massaging their cheek area in small circles and stroking from their temple down along the jawbone (*Figure 43*).

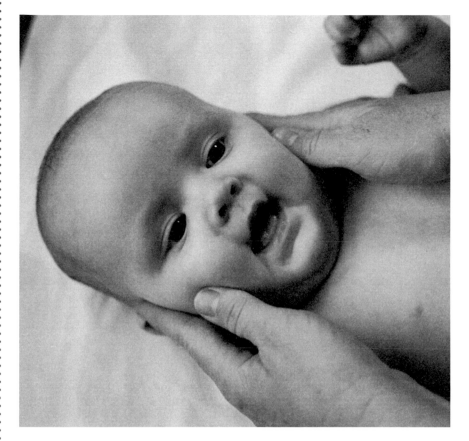

Figure 43

Susan Harley

Chapter Nine

CONCLUSION

Now that you have reached the end of this book, I hope that it brings you to the beginning of a new, gentle, and touching relationship with your children. Use this book to guide you, to inspire you, and to help you to create a loving and connected relationships with those you touch, especially your children. Nurture them, grow them, love them and inspire them, through your touch, to be the best they can be, as you model being the best you can be.

Remember the many benefits of massaging your children:

Benefits for the child:

- Promotes parent-child bonding and communication.
- Promotes brain growth.
- Increases physical growth and development.
- Promotes good self-esteem.
- Improves digestion, respiratory, and circulatory systems.

Susan Harley

Helps relieve discomfort from colic, gas, diarrhea, congestion, and teething.

Improves immune system and decreases production of stress hormones.

Benefits for parents:

Aids parents in helping their child relax in times of stress.

Reduces stress of a parent who is separated from their child during the day.

Helps parents learn and respond appropriately to child's non-verbal clues.

Promotes confidence and competence in caring for their child.

Improves parent-child bonding and communication.

A FUN and RELAXING time for parent and child.

Remember to breathe, to keep softening your touch, to look into your children's eyes, to talk to them, and to let your hands be GENTLE HANDS as they transmit your love and help your children grow.

REFERENCES AND SUGGESTED READINGS

Brazelton, T. B. (1993) *Touchpoints: The essential reference guide to your child's behavioral development.* Doubleday, Sydney.

Field, T.M. (1995) *Massage therapy for infants and children.* Journal of Developmental and Behavioral Pediatrics, 16, 105-111.

Field, T.M. (1998) *Massage therapy effect.* American Psychological Association, 53, 1270-1281.

Field, T.M., Grizzle, N., Scafidi, F., Abrams, S. and S.R. (1996a) *Massage Therapy for infants of depressed mothers.* Infant Behavior and Development, 19, 109-114.

Field, T. M., Seligman, S., Scafidy, F. and Schanberg, S. (1996b) *Alleviating Post-traumatic stress in children*

following Hurrican Andrew. Journal of Applied

Developmental Psychology, 17, 37-50.

Health Department of Western Australia (1986) *The Book of
the Child.* Perth, WA.

Kabat-Zinn, M. and Kabat-Zinn, J. (1997) *Everyday
Blessings: the Inner Work of Mindful Parenting.* Hyperion,
New York.

Scafidi, F.A., Field, T.M. and Schanberg, S.M. (1990)
Massage stimulates growth in preterm infants. Infant
Behavior and Development, 13, 167-188.

Sears, W. and Sears, M. (1993) *The Baby Book.* Little Brown
& Co.